MUSAFIRAH
The Faithful Traveler

By
Aisha bint David

PROLOGUE

This story is of a woman's journey to becoming a Muslim, a wife, and a well-seasoned teacher, all while traveling and moving to various cities in the USA, as well as other countries. Her faith journey begins when she hits rock bottom after realizing that her years of study and hard work have somehow led her to a life of emptiness, so she decides to start over at the age of twenty-six. The events that follow her brave decision make for an extraordinary story of hope and faith.

DEDICATION

This book is dedicated to my parents; two ordinary people with tremendous talent who led surprisingly courageous lives. My mother believed I could do anything, go anywhere, and overcome any challenge. For this reason, I never felt afraid to try a new path, take a new job, or follow my dreams. To my father, whose bravery protected thousands and whose love protected the heart of a little girl. May you be rewarded with goodness for every sacrifice. I pray that one day you too will join me on this incredible faith journey, Amin.

Lovingly,
Your daughter - Hilarie Leigh Clement (Aka: Aisha Bint David)

40TH HADITH - TRANSLATION

On the authority of Ibn Umar (R.A.), who said: The Messenger of Allah (S.A.W.) took me by the shoulder and said:
"Be in this world as though you were a stranger or a traveler/wayfarer." (Sahih al Bukhari)

ABOUT THE AUTHOR

Aisha Bint David is the commonly used name of Hilarie Clement, who also goes by "Um Youcef" (mother of Youcef in the Arabic language.) Aisha lives in the capital city of North Carolina with her husband and six children. She's been teaching for over 25 years in the areas of French language, ESL/EFL, English language, Elementary subjects, and Social Studies. After leaving her hometown in 1997, she discovered Islam and converted/reverted then married and started her travels. She's lived in France, several cities in the USA, the United Arab Emirates, and Saudi Arabia, and vacationed in Algeria, Oman, and Canada. Aisha enjoys long walks on cool evenings, crocheting blankets, and international, travel. She's also a small business owner. You can find her on social media (Sadoun & Co LLC.) She loves receiving feedback and fan mail!

TABLE OF CONTENTS

Chapter 1: 1
   Becoming Like a Newborn Baby Again

Chapter 2: 5
   Pre-Islam

Chapter 3: 9
   My First Year as a Muslim (Academic Year 1998-1999), in Dubai

Chapter 4: 12
   Motherhood at Last

Chapter 5: 16
   9/11 (2001)

Chapter 6: 20
   Chicago

Chapter 7: 24
   Saudi Arabia

Chapter 8: 28
   COVID-19

Chapter 9: 30
   A New Chapter Begins, on May 13, 2021

Chapter 10: 32
   Epilogue

MUSAFIRAH: Comprehension Check 34

1
BECOMING LIKE A NEWBORN BABY AGAIN

The week had ended, and it was finally time to take the next step as she could no longer delay or deny her new identity. "How am I going to tell my family about this?" She thought to herself. Emotions were racing and many fears came into her mind as she excitedly drove to the red brick building on Ligon Street in Raleigh. She was unsure who to ask or how to explain her request, but she tried to figure out the details while driving. Over and over she repeated the words she had committed to memory, a turn here, a stop sign there, she was practicing the "kalima', the Muslim declaration of faith. She was bursting with joy and excitement.

It was a steamy Friday night and she was still adjusting to this new pattern of Friday nights. Gone were the days of visiting bars, and clubs, listening to music, and having a few cocktails. Friday nights were now spent going to coffee shops or the mall. Some weeks she was content just staying home and reading from the mountain of library books. She had almost completed the year; a new life in a growing city, far away from family. Everything had seemed to fall into place, however, she wasn't accustomed to such warm summer nights in May. Ironically, it was a pleasant change. The seasons were different and so was her outlook on life. She was ready to jump into the deep end, just as she desperately wished the community pool was open late on this particularly warm Friday night.

She entered the red brick building in her newly purchased modest clothing, feeling nervous but ready. The room was full of women, laughing and talking. Who could she ask? Nobody seemed to be in charge, rather, it felt more like a party than a "ladies' gathering" for a lecture. They were all here to enjoy themselves, and meet friends. It almost felt like a family reunion though clearly these ladies were not related to one another. She observed quietly and then proceeded.

"I would like to speak with someone about becoming a Muslim" she whispered to one of the many women whose eyes seemed especially kind and welcoming. "SISTERS! SISTERS! Please listen carefully! We have a new 'shehada' tonight! Please come forward and be a witness to her testimony of faith!" All eyes were now fixed squarely on the young woman.

She had announced it so loudly and with such joy and certainty! Was she going to go through with this? In front of all these strangers? It was supposed to be a private affair, behind closed doors, with low voices and just a few people. It wasn't at all how she had imagined this to be, but now in the spotlight, she knew it was now or never.

First was the difficult task of donning the hijab. Strangers would know of her new identity. Now it was the act of publicly declaring her faith. There must have been fifty of them, just staring impatiently at the frightened stranger. Just then she remembered the encouragement and the reward of taking one's "shehada"; when you say these words, and declare your Islam, you become like a newborn baby, free of sin. Your life is a "tabula rasa," and your new book of deeds would begin at that moment. She exhaled deeply. She had certainly found what she was longing for back in New York. The emptiness had been replaced with hope.

Thankfully it was only women and there was no microphone. Several women stood close to her and she was grateful, as she might have just passed out from the heat or the intense fear swelling up in her chest. "I want you to repeat these words after me, so listen carefully." She began, *"Ash hadu- an-Lah - Ila ha- Ila Lah. Wa Ash hadu anna Muhammadan abduhu wa rasuluhu." There is only One God (worthy of worship) with no partners, and Muhammad is His Slave and Messenger.* (This is the 'kalima' which new Muslims say to enter Islam.)

Not even seconds after repeating the words the room exploded with "TAKBEER!" "ALLAHU AKBAR." She then repeated the "shahada" (testimony of faith) in English as well, until she got to the part about Prophet Muhammad (peace be upon him), when suddenly she burst into tears, uncontrollable heartfelt sobs. She continued until the end, crying like a baby in front of all those unknown ladies, shamelessly allowing herself to feel every ounce of release and joy. She couldn't help it. It had been a solid 8 months since she had started this journey in solitude. The mere mention of the name, Prophet Muhammad (peace be upon him), evoked deep emotions that came pouring out of her, like water from a faucet. She remembered his (peace be upon him) life of struggle, his sad childhood, the emotional and physical pain throughout his sixty-three years, and his many sacrifices. Would she now have to give up her family and loved ones to be a Muslim too? It didn't matter now, she was a Muslim and she was at peace.

One by one the sisters hugged her, kissed her, cried with her, and encouraged her to be strong. She wanted to put her face to the floor and thank Allah for this tremendous blessing, but it was not yet time to pray and the line of ladies seemed endless. One enthusiastic sister held her tightly like a mother holding her child. "I am Samira. I am your sister from Algeria. I want to know you and be your friend so please give me your phone number." She wasn't sure why someone would go to this much trouble, waiting in line and then insisting on following up, but she handed over the number on a small scrap of paper. Eventually, the call to prayer was made. At long last, she was ready to perform her first "salah" (Muslim prayer) inside the mosque, with other sisters, no longer alone at home.

She left the mosque late that night with no concept of time, completely exhausted and yet, feeling as light as a feather. Somehow her mind and body were floating. Without a care in the world, she drove home, tears streaming happily down her cheeks, triumphant that she had found the courage to follow her heart. The night was still warm and a soft breeze mixed with sprinkles left her feeling fresh and clean, despite the exhaustion and the sweat. "How will I tell my roommate? What will mom think of all this?" She thought, but surprisingly wasn't worried anymore. What seemed important now was this new sense of freedom, like starting life all over again, only this time she had a guidebook and her heart was the compass. The physical change was minimal whereas the spiritual and emotional metamorphosis was grand. She had a new mission statement. She was utterly focused on pleasing the Creator of the Universe.

As the weeks and months passed, that feeling only intensified. The routine of praying five times a day became easier and she looked forward to it despite her difficulty pronouncing the Arabic words. Her clothing became more comfortable and buying food without pork or alcohol became more natural. She had met with her new friend, Samira, who introduced her to other American Muslim sisters. Soon she would be ready for marriage and then an unexpected move overseas. Eventually, her life would become so full that twenty-four hours seemed insufficient to juggle everything. Years turned into decades and eventually, she would return to the red brick building. Her future visits, however, would be made with other people and not solo. Her journey in life with a Muslim identity had just begun.

2

PRE-ISLAM

My roots are European and I'm originally from New York State. Before knowing anything about Islam, my life was as typical as any American girl could be. My family celebrated Christian-American holidays and birthdays, my grandparents visited every year, we spent summers camping, and I did loads of babysitting. I waited tables in my late teens and moved away to live on campus during my college years. Eventually, I completed my education and started a career as a public school teacher.

It wasn't too long before I realized that teaching was truly an emotionally exhausting job. Plus, the heavy winters in Central New York made for a cold and lonely life, despite living close to my parents. I had slipped into a severe, clinical depression. My new objective was to start my life again in another state, with, perhaps, another career. I couldn't bear the fact that after putting in six years at college, I was now questioning my very existence and the purpose of life. I was in a funk and nothing seemed to help, aside from one therapist named Ruth. She was probably the first person I had ever met who would tell me the truth, to my face, knowing that it would hurt my feelings. She was the person I most trusted. Thankfully, I took her heartfelt advice.

In the summer of 1997, I left New York. It was the last day of school and my car was already packed. I moved to North Carolina with a dear college friend. She was ready for the sunshine and I was excited to hit the beach! We quickly found jobs and set up our apartment. We had been roommates in France during a semester-long study abroad, so sharing a flat was like re-living the good old days. Somehow though, my life still seemed meaningless. I attended services at several local churches, immersed myself in exercise, and took on various odd jobs. I also found myself drowning in debt. Eventually, I started teaching again. Wake County had me teaching remedial reading for middle schoolers each morning, and the same for elementary students every afternoon. Wake Tech Community College hired me to teach ESL (English as a Second Language) to adults at night. It was there that I would learn the meaning of destiny. Additionally, this job would lay the foundation for my future career of teaching adults and give my life some fulfillment and joy.

Many adult students at the college tried to become friendly with staff as they needed help with job applications or immigration paperwork. One student in particular would show up to campus early each evening, looking for help with the computers, namely, the internet, as that was new and exciting in the late 1990s. Even having an email account was a commodity, especially for someone who spoke little English. On many occasions he would be sitting near my work area, staring at the computer screen as if it held some important secrets. I would help him, reluctantly, by creating an email account for him and showing him how to finish his homework. He would speak in broken English and use up what little time I had left before going in to teach my students.

Sometimes I was annoyed by his constant presence however, he was a motivated student and seemed eager to progress. He wasn't **my** student, however, he insisted on getting help from **only me**, because I had a unique skill that the other teachers did not have. I spoke French fluently, and he was a French-speaking Algerian. He would later teach me the basics of Islam and eventually become my husband.

Sometimes I would contemplate how content he seemed in his simple life. He was sharing a tiny apartment with his brothers and friends. They worked non-stop and yet, they all got along so well. They were clean, respectful, and welcoming. One day I decided to investigate the religion he had told me about. The most readily available information about Islam focused on the many prohibitions: pork, alcohol, drugs, listening to music, and others.

I started to research each, one by one, from ordinary library books, hoping to find some benefits of these so-called "prohibitions" so that I could prove to this "foreigner" and "ESL student" just how mistaken he was. I truly thought he was brainwashed. What could be so terrible about hot dogs? Why couldn't I enjoy a wine cooler twice a week? Ironically, one by one, I realized the dangers of each prohibition. So I gave up pork and alcohol almost immediately after researching the facts. Eventually, I would read about the dangers of usury and cut up all my credit cards too. Not only that, I started to read about the scientific benefits of praying, fasting, and doing charity work. This led me to read books about Islam until finally, I was ready to read the Quran. This search continued until I reached a true identity crisis. Insomnia crept in and I could no longer live with myself. I had to decide once and for all what I truly believed.

Interestingly, the hijab was the most difficult aspect to accept. After all, I had spent time, money, and energy to dress well, stay fit, and look my best! Why would God ask me to cover up His beautiful creation? It was the last change I had to make but the hardest. Although I had accepted everything from the concept of "Tawheed" (belief in the One God) to performing the five daily prayers, on time and in any setting, and although I had even tried fasting, there was an indescribable fear that if I could not practice every aspect, then I truly could not call myself a Muslim. Eventually, I started my own "homemade hijab wardrobe." This consisted of fabric being cut into square shapes for scarves, and buying my clothes two sizes larger. It became easier with time. Later in my journey, I would start my own Muslim-friendly clothing business as it had been so difficult to find modest apparel that first year as a Muslim. I wished every Muslim would one day be able to purchase modest clothing with just as much ease as we could when buying a pair of jeans.

What was different about Islam? I could have remained a Christian and followed along with any church. It didn't have to be the Catholic Church, the one I was raised in. However, Islam was unique. There was God, and then messengers, and then everyone else. It was crystal clear. There are five pillars and six articles of faith. It was easy enough for even a child to understand and yet, putting it all into practice, simultaneously, while leaving off any one single aspect would certainly lead to hypocrisy. I felt that denying any part of Islam or neglecting any aspect of it would result in me living a photocopy of my Christian life. It had to be all or nothing. So when I was finally accustomed to wearing the hijab and convinced about its importance, I decided to take my "shahada." My depression was long gone and my life had completely changed. In my heart, I knew this was my destiny, my homecoming, and my purpose in life was finally clear.

3

MY FIRST YEAR AS A MUSLIM (ACADEMIC YEAR 1998-1999), IN DUBAI

Nothing could have prepared me for that first breath of sweltering, heavy humid air in late August in the well-known city of Dubai, in the United Arab Emirates. Never had I experienced this kind of heat in all my life! It was unbearable, especially in summer. When the airplane landed and all passengers prepared to exit, there was a rush of excitement! Here I was in the land of a Muslim-majority, ready to meet the school representative who would chauffeur me to the "Golden Sands" studio apartments and prepare me for a year of elementary teaching at Al Ittihad School. I was the new third-grade homeroom teacher. I hadn't felt that much excitement since attending my first college classes. It was something completely new and different.

From the day I took my shahada in May, until the day I landed in Dubai, everything felt like a fast-paced Hollywood movie. I was engaged by the end of June, married by the end of July, packing my bags, and saying goodbye to family members in August. The hardest part was waving goodbye to my newlywed husband at JFK airport. Additionally, I had missed my best friend's wedding. I had given up the lease on our freshly-painted one-bedroom apartment. I had apologized for backing out of the French Language teaching position at a public middle school in Raleigh. My plans for a quiet first year of marriage were replaced with a new goal; paying off my student loans. I also wanted to learn some Arabic and looked forward to having a classroom. I had packed my entire life into two suitcases and apologized to all my loved ones. Thoughts raced through my mind while exiting the airplane, and my body felt a tremendous fatigue, an insatiable thirst, That is how I first entered the continent of Asia.

The first few days in Dubai were fascinating. They reminded me of my semester In France. It was my junior year of college. That experience allowed me to live amongst non-English speakers and see a bit of diversity, but walking the streets of Dubai felt like another planet! Every skin color imaginable was apparent, every language was heard, and every type of clothing was worn. It was overwhelming and intoxicating and I couldn't get enough of this city. The white sand, the transparent water, the mesmerizing open-air markets, and all the hustle and bustle were exhilarating.

All I could compare it to was New York City. How did it feel when the early European immigrants were trying to maneuver around that iconic American city, buy groceries, and communicate with people? English was the common language but newcomers could not yet speak it. In Dubai, in 1998, only twenty percent of the population were Emirati and the majority of people were migrants from the Indian subcontinent working mostly blue-collar jobs so they spoke any number of languages. Mostly everyone knew a bit of Arabic. The taxi drivers were of keen interest as they seemed to be the eyes and ears of the city. My senses were on high alert! Every outing became an adventure, and every morning I awoke to the melodious chorus of the "muadthaan" (the person who announces the time for prayer for Muslims five times a day.) My mind was doing better than my body as it took many weeks to acclimatize and learn proper hydration. I observed everything and listened attentively while outside the apartment. That allowed me to take in an incredible amount of information. It took many hours of writing and reflection to process everything so I kept a journal and recorded events religiously so as not to forget.

Third grade was probably the perfect age for me to start my career as an elementary classroom teacher, or "homeroom" teacher as they called it. The Al-Ittihad campus looked, at first, a bit run down having limited resources, however, when students showed up on their first day, the school had somehow transformed into an international, world-class institution. Later, the school opened several more state-of-the-art campuses in Dubai and other Emirates. I had never seen so many brand new, shiny sport utility vehicles (SUVs) in one place, in my entire life. It was the most luxurious carpooling line I could have ever imagined, but this was just another day in the life of my students. Mothers and caretakers began escorting their children to the freshly decorated classrooms. Drivers parked and waited patiently. They seemed to have their unique schedules tool, meeting other drivers while smiling and chatting over a cup of Arabic "Qahwa" (coffee) and enjoying freshly rinsed dates. The other teachers and I welcomed our students happily as the academic year was about to begin.

Not only did I meet some of the kindest people that year, but I also found support in those incredible friends with whom I still keep in touch, twenty-six years later. It would be a year of learning, teaching, adventure, and paying off tens of thousands of dollars. My student loans and other debts were always in the back of my mind. It would also be a year spent living alone, aside from three weeks when my husband visited me. My students and their families took me under their wing, and shared their culture and history with me, often inviting me on weekends to the desert or the beach or lavish gatherings in their beautiful homes. Little did I know that my first year in Dubai would set the foundation for a life of teaching, traveling, and even preparation for motherhood. Dubai was nothing like I had imagined yet, it far exceeded my expectations. When the academic year ended, I tearfully handed in my resignation. It was time to go back home. I was ready to start my married life and live as a Muslim, in my own country. The many lessons I had gained in Dubai that year would remain with me forever.

4

MOTHERHOOD AT LAST

Upon my arrival in New York City, my husband met me with a beautiful bouquet. We drove as far East as we could that day and spent the night at a cheap hotel. I could not describe my range of feelings: joy at returning home to the familiarity, relief at reuniting with my husband, sadness from missing new friends and reminiscing about my lovely students, excitement in finding a new teaching job, and hope... Would motherhood ever happen to me? I was approaching thirty years of age and still had those debts weighing me down.

I am the eldest of my siblings and the last to marry. At times I felt that perhaps I would never become a mother. In reality, Allah was just delaying me, and preparing me for the enormous responsibility I would later have. As usual, my impatience would get the best of me. So I put these worries out of my head and focused on paying off the rest of my student loans. There was no reason to delay this objective and I certainly did not want to work if I had a baby! So, I applied for a job at the local Islamic school in Raleigh, NC. Ironically, I was interviewing at the same red brick building where I had taken my shahada, but this visit was completely different. This time I had elementary school teaching experience and overseas living experience. I was excited to share all I had learned in exchange for paying off all my debt. Once again, I prepared my classroom and eagerly awaited my new students.

The school was so overjoyed to have a certified teacher, a practicing Muslim, whose native tongue was English, that they piled on the classes. I was the fourth-grade homeroom teacher. I was also the fifth and seventh-grade Language Arts teacher. It was flattering but impossible. I did my best and immersed myself in my newest roles, however, I could barely stay awake past seven o'clock. Perhaps I was overwhelmed and just needed to drink more coffee. Everything suddenly tasted strange and I had no appetite. My body was also quite weak. Maybe it was the fatigue of setting up our apartment and starting a new job. I simply could not understand what was happening to me.

Barely a week of school had passed when the morning sickness started. New mothers are so interesting to observe when they realize their bodies are not acting normally. The excitement is overwhelming and time seems to drag on forever. I was no different from any other first-time mom-to-be. How could this happen? I had just signed a contract for the academic year and was extremely close to paying off those debts.

Despite the fatigue, I stuck with the original plan and went to work each day, dealing with the nausea and coping with the exhaustion. My husband would drop me off and pick me up daily, so clearly he felt sorry but was also eager for me to finish what I had started. He could have paid the debts, but I wanted to do it myself. The Master's and Bachelor's degrees were mine and nobody could take them away from me, so I felt it was only fair that I should pay for them. Every morning I struggled to get out of bed. I kept crackers and ginger ale on my nightstand. Every afternoon I had a nap. My mother had encouraged me to keep working for as long as possible and she called often which always boosted my morale.

Ironically, the physical struggle was only part of it. I was simply way too eager to have that baby in my arms! My library books were pushed to the bottom of my nightstand, making room for the new assortment of literature on pregnancy and motherhood. During my first year of marriage, my husband and I lived in separate countries. Our second year of marriage was an emotional rollercoaster of highs, lows, and throwing up. Incidentally, my husband was also in shock and overwhelmed with fear and excitement at the news of our baby. He was working many hours to save money. I was surprised at how mundane life could be despite the excitement of becoming a parent! I was learning to balance everything from people to plans to a healthy lifestyle. The nine months seemed to drag on forever but finally, the debts were paid.

At long last, Youcef arrived in May of 2000. I hadn't been able to complete the school year and this was my only regret; leaving my job and my adorable students two months shy of summer vacation. Caring for baby Youcef each day was like opening a gift I had been waiting for my entire life. Motherhood was more painful, exhausting, and, emotionally overwhelming than anticipated, but it quickly became the most wonderful aspect. My perspective on life shifted one-hundred and eighty degrees. With my debts finally paid, and the school year done, my heart longed for Dubai. So in August of 2000, we returned to the UAE. This time it was all three of us. I wasn't there to pay off debts, or to learn the basics of Islam. This time I wanted to experience life as a wife, mother, and teacher, within the context of a Muslim-majority. So I taught in Dubai but lived in Sharjah, the family-friendly Emirate. We bought a used car and settled into the school accommodation, hoping to feel settled and content. My hopes were high.

This time around in Dubai, however, life was more challenging. Youcef was just 4 months old when I started teaching that fall. Al Ittihad School put me as the first-grade teacher instead of the third grade. I felt like a fish out of water. I cried with my students some days, frustrated at teaching them how to read English when they could barely get by in their native Arabic tongue. Teaching ESL for adults was a pleasure but teaching children felt like torture! I had to learn from my colleagues that year and my Arabic improved significantly as a result. Sadly, family life was not as I had anticipated either. My husband traveled every two months for immigration and I felt like a single-married mom. It was a valuable experience however, I was completely exhausted and by the end of June, I was expecting again, much to my surprise. Once again I tearfully handed in my resignation and we headed back home to North Carolina. I was grateful for the two fabulous years in Dubai, however, now I longed to be a stay-at-home mom and focus on family life. We flew to NY and visited family but my little adventures would soon be coming to an end. Little did I know that everything was about to change and that we would live through one of the worst events in modern history.

5

9/11 (2001)

Back in Raleigh my husband had rented us a one-bedroom flat. It was the very end of August and we decided on a 6-month lease, hoping to save money and eventually move into a two-bedroom apartment after the baby was born. Having Youcef, and baby number two on the way, made us confident that we should now settle in the USA. Teaching could wait a year or even longer! I thoroughly enjoyed the routine of taking care of my toddler Youcef. Immigration was backed up and my husband had already interviewed for his green card years prior (even before we got married), but living overseas and continuously changing addresses did not help his situation. He was still waiting for his green card status so we checked the mailbox daily and focused on a more traditional role-based marriage. I wanted to learn more about parenting. We settled quickly into life at "Spanish Trace" apartments. My suitcases were packed away.

Thankfully, the morning sickness was much better. I started pushing Youcef in his stroller for daily walks. I enjoyed meeting old friends and colleagues. Grocery store trips were the highlight of my week and Youcef enjoyed all the attention as strangers often admired his gorgeous curls. Life was simple and I truly felt happy. I quickly settled into my new role; preparing meals, reading bedtime stories to my son, and meeting other stay-at-home moms. Life seemed too good to be true. Dubai was a distant memory and I was content in our little apartment.

It was the morning of 9/11/2001. I had gone out to do the grocery shopping, when suddenly I felt the stares of a hundred people. They were not looking at Youcef this time, they were looking directly at me, and my hijab. TV announcers repeatedly accused *Muslim terrorists* of declaring war on the USA constantly showing the horrific scenes of airplanes crashing into the iconic Twin Towers in NYC. I paid the cashier quickly and drove home sobbing, still unsure about what I had just witnessed. Youcef was singing happily in the back seat, unaware. My husband was home resting on the sofa, oblivious to the news.

"Turn on the TV!" I shouted. Like every other American that day, we were in a state of shock. Friends from Dubai started calling and emailing to check on us. My father called too, explaining that repercussions would be made for this type of action. I could sense the fear in his voice, understandably worried about his pregnant daughter venturing out with a baby, in full hijab. He was right. Ever so swiftly, the US military would soon be stationed in Afghanistan. Gone were the days of feeling like a confident hijab-clad Muslim woman. I felt sick knowing that we had traded in the safety of life in the UAE for what would soon become an unpredictable and dangerously discriminative United States of America.

Over days and weeks, our happy moments became sour ones. Immigration had put everything on hold for many Muslims, including my husband. His days working at Manpower were over. He had to find employment elsewhere. I frantically started looking for a teaching job overseas, but the school year had already begun. Besides, this baby was due in February, so how would I manage? For the first time, I felt afraid to leave my home and live in my own country. I stayed at home most of the time, only taking Youcef on occasional walks or waiting for my husband's day off to do the shopping as a family instead of going with Youcef. Life for Muslims in 2001 was frightening. I turned inward for support and started teaching myself some of the Quran from where I had left off in Dubai. I began teaching myself Arabic too, using what I had already mastered, going over each letter and each word a little at a time. It was challenging but rewarding. I also started to miss ESL teaching so I registered for a class online through Shenandoah University: English Linguistics 101. That course proved to be of great benefit to me as a teacher years later. I started to understand the meaning of Surah Al-Baqarah, verse 216 when Allah says, "But perhaps you hate a thing and it is good for you; and perhaps you love a thing and it is bad for you. And Allah Knows, while you know not". (Quran) It had been a tough year but much good had come out of it including the birth of my first little dolly. The second delivery was much easier as I already knew what to expect, having gone through delivery once.

Fatima was born fifteen days early, in the same hospital room as Youcef. Dad and Cheri came down to visit from Washington DC. My mom's cousin and her daughter visited as well. My sister came with her family. Mom came later when Fatima was about a month old as she always felt new moms and new babies needed some time to adjust.

We moved to a beautiful two-bedroom apartment My life was bittersweet. The excitement and joy of having another baby overshadowed the sadness and the constant fear I was feeling. Hubby was working hard and I appreciated the time at home. I had not anticipated working for a long time but my destiny was about to take me out of the situation once again. The fear was closing in on me and I was open to anything, as long as I could push my babies in a stroller without having to look over my shoulder every few minutes. My home life would soon be traded in for a classroom once more.

We left the USA on Fatima's first birthday as I could no longer live in perpetual fear. I felt like an estranged citizen in my own country. I explained this to my family but how could they fully understand? I didn't want to burden them with my fears or problems. I was the only Muslim in my family. There was only one choice, I had to get my family to a place where I felt safe. The new school was in Sharjah. It was called the "Creative School of Science." My husband was also ready for a change. His Green Card had arrived one summer day. With it came a newfound sense of freedom. Nowadays he could exit the USA for six months at a time. Traveling only twice a year seemed perfectly acceptable to me. So I started teaching again, this time 4th grade boys as the homeroom teacher. I was determined to stay out of the USA and felt grateful that I had an option, unlike many others who stayed and suffered with the situation.

Once again, my husband and I drove to JFK airport, our 2 little ones in the back. We would enjoy another 4 years in the UAE, and I would give birth twice more; once in Sharjah and once in Al Ain. My career path would change as I started teaching adults ESL and EFL (English as a Foreign Language), and we felt settled, happy, thriving, and safe! Sadly, my husband was still traveling to safeguard his green card status. He would work for a couple of months and return to the UAE. It was the price we paid for our life overseas. In my mind, there was no way I would go back to America. By this point in time, the USA had invaded Iraq and there were many scandals from the war along with evidence showing that the events on 9/11/2001 were obscure.

In February of 2007, my husband insisted that we visit the USA because his citizenship interview was approaching. I was missing my parents and wanted to introduce the two new additions to our family, however, the thought of getting stuck in the USA frightened me. The idea of visiting made me uncomfortable but my husband assured me this would be a short trip. He reminded me that once he had his citizenship the traveling would stop and somehow I felt that our lives would be more stable. So we flew to NYC and spent a wonderful vacation with family in New York. We had planned our two-and-a-half-week vacation perfectly. Allah had other plans. **"We plan, Allah plans, Allah is the best of planners." (Quran, 8:30)**

6

CHICAGO

It had been a few days since the heart-breaking interview with immigration in Chicago, I was still recovering from the shock. His citizenship was rejected for the second time in a row. He was out of the country often and they said his days in the USA were insufficient. The residue from 9/11 was still lingering and Muslims living in America were still under the microscope in 2006, five years after that horrible day.

"How could they NOT give you citizenship? You are married to an American citizen. You have 4 children who are also citizens!" I wanted to scream but doing so would not help. We were stuck! My fears had been realized and there was absolutely nothing I could do about it.

The trusted sheikh (Muslim advisor) had advised me to take this trip, to see my parents, and to follow my husband. He firmly assured me that if we did get stuck for any reason, I would have to accept everything. He was my husband, after all. Returning to the UAE as a single mom, with 4 kids under five was not even negotiable. I could barely handle them all on my own when my husband was close by, so how would I do this alone? My hubby returned to the Emirates alone and sold off or gave away everything I had spent the past four years accumulating. It was heart-breaking, but a perfect reminder of the reality of life: you can't take any of it with you when you die, only your deeds. From that experience, I learned to invest more wisely in the afterlife, and not be so focused on accumulating wealth or material items.

It is said there are 7 heavens and 8 doors of paradise. Maybe, I thought, this was the perfect time to serve my parents and earn the door called "serving one's parents." I insisted that we stay in New York and re-apply for his citizenship. It was an opportunity for me to spend time with my own family. I could look for teaching jobs there. But my husband was like a fish out of water. He had nothing to do in my hometown and longed for some semblance of what we had in North Carolina. My kids were not used to life in America, especially the weather in my hometown. After several months of trying to settle down there, the situation was bleak. I could not secure any teaching job and my husband had started working with his brothers in Chicago. We had nearly run out of savings. My family was busy with their own lives and it became obvious that my door to paradise would not be linked to my parents. I would have to put all my eggs into the basket, called "raising righteous children" instead of "serving parents." After all, I had four of them already and wasn't planning to have another. They were as eager as me to have my full attention so I prayed hard, made my intention, and took the deep dive into following my husband. It was terrifying yet exciting and it felt like our only option.

My husband had 3 brothers in Chicago so that was the logical place to settle. With the little money we had left from the Emirates, we moved to the North Side and rented a 2 bedroom flat from an Algerian family who would eventually become very dear to us. I still longed for the UAE but quickly found a job teaching fourth grade at a local Islamic school. My kids were happy and made friends easily but what excited them the most was having cousins close by. Chicago had its share of good and bad days but I still felt unsafe as a Muslim living in America. We had walked several times to a local park and had rocks thrown at us and were called "terrorists" on top of that. The discrimination was much better than before however I worried constantly for my kids and me, anytime we left the house. I also felt overwhelmed taking the four of them outside anywhere. My husband worked 60 to 70 hours a week and once again I felt like a single-married mom, but this is not unusual for immigrants who support large families. I had become like an immigrant in my own country except that I was an American citizen. I was the minority in my circle of friends, English was now my second language. Days were long, filled with the difficult responsibility of caring for my growing family.

Another baby boy was added to our family that year. He was born during a terrible snowstorm, a few days shy of Christmas. The cold and wind of Chicago were even worse than that of my hometown, and once again, that old familiar feeling crept in. I knew in my heart that we would not settle in Chicago. My husband had finally become a naturalized American citizen so I started my search for jobs in Sharjah and Dubai. Little did I know that we would only return to the UAE as visitors one day, not as residents. The world was experiencing an economic crisis and unemployment was high in many countries. My heart broke all over again. I was sure we would be stuck there for the rest of our lives, until I remembered the trusted sheikh, once again.

He had advised me to never give up my dream of "Al-hijrah." I desperately wanted to leave my homeland in search of a better Muslim environment for the kids, and a safer one for our family. It seemed impossible with five kids, however, I started to notice there were many jobs in Saudi Arabia. So I applied for jobs in Saudi Arabia. They seemed to have an abundance of teaching jobs and they were keen to hire native English speakers.

Eventually, the job offers poured in from big cities like Madina, Riyadh, and Jeddah. The Kingdom of Saudi Arabia seemed a bit intimidating as women could not yet drive and we would all need a residency visa to stay there, unlike their lenient neighbors in the UAE, where all you needed to enter was an American passport. Visas could be made on the spot, unlike the strict Saudi immigration system, requiring a police check, medical report, and other documents to earn residency. Several months passed and the offers were solid but my residency visa never came through. The new school year had already begun so I focused on raising my five kids and tried to brace myself for another autumn, another winter, and another year of being patient. Ramadan was rapidly approaching so I put all the Saudi paperwork on hold and focused on the task at hand: meals, cleaning, homework, and laundry! I exhaled deeply and prayed for a solution. Truly, what Allah had planned for me would exceed my expectations. It was simply a matter of time before my patience was rewarded. (94:5) Indeed, there is ease with hardship. **(94:6) Most certainly, there is ease with hardship. (Quran 94:5-6)**

7

SAUDI ARABIA

Truly, when something is written for you, it will not miss you. If it's not meant for you, it will never happen. That's how I came to understand the concept of destiny. How many times have I learned this lesson since becoming a Muslim? At this point in my life, I was sure that we were truly stuck in Chicago. Who was willing to hire a mother of five, who barely spoke Arabic, with a now probably moldy Master's degree, and in need of 7 residency visas? I had all but given up.

Life in Chicago was challenging, but I was happy to stay at home with my kids, walk them to school each day, drive a minivan, and feel somewhat settled. Aside from the anti-muslim propaganda, and the horrible cold, I thought this was as good as it could get for us.

The situation for Muslim Americans was not great, but it was much better in 2009 than in 2001. Barack Obama had become president. My kids were attending Quran classes every evening and I hoped life would get better with time. My biggest challenge now was dealing with the public schools. CPS, or Chicago Public School (District.) They had their fair share of Muslims, as well as a nationally recognized reputation for gangs, drugs, crimes, weapons, and ranking in the bottom ten states regarding test scores. As an educator, it bothered me, but what choice did I have? Private schooling was out of the question financially. Homeschooling was impossible with all these kids (I actually homeschooled Youcef for 1 full year.) So I decided that patience and prayer would be my most useful tools to find a solution. They were.

The email seemed fake at first. Taif University....ELC....immediate employment....lecturer position. Was I dreaming? My husband quickly confirmed that Taif was just an hour's drive from Makkah. My reply to his email was a resounding YES. My physical was up-to-date, as well as my police report. All I needed was the final visa application. Then I needed to pack up our entire lives into 12 suitcases, and 7 backpacks. It happened so quickly that mostly everything was left behind. Our kind landlord and his wife took over, and put everything to good use, either giving it away or discarding it as needed. Truly Allah is the Most Wise, the Most Kind, and the best of planners; if only we would recognize that in our daily lives, we would never lose sleep or be worried about anything in life. I felt like I was dreaming and I didn't want to wake up from it.

We left the Chicago O-Hare airport on Halloween night, 2009, and found ourselves riding up the infamous Taif Road; a steep, winding, mountainous terrain on all sides. The beautiful agricultural city would become our newest home and I would enjoy three years of teaching at Taif University. We performed "Hajj" in 2011 and went many times for "Umrah" (the lesser pilgrimage.) Also, in Taif, we would be blessed with one more baby, a beautiful little dolly who was named after the doctor who delivered her. Our family was complete, but the story doesn't end there.

As many business transactions take place over a cup of tea and a hearty conversation, I would eventually be offered a teaching position in Makkah, for a job I had never applied for. As Allah would have it, my dreams of settling in the Emirates were simply a preparation. Allah had intended for us to reach the city of Makkah instead, where I would teach at Umm al Qura University in the English Language Center. In short, my resume had been passed over to the ELC in Makkah, by someone who knew someone. I happily and humbly accepted the offer immediately. I learned the lesson of networking and how every person you meet has a role in your life, just as you play a role in theirs. It was another reminder to remain hopeful in life.

Once again I remembered the sheikh, who had already, sadly, passed away in the city of Madina, whose advice had served me well: "Remain steadfast and stick with the original affair." His words remained fresh in my mind. "When you have the intention for something, be sure Allah will test you with it" He was correct in all his advice. "Give glad tidings to the patient persevering ones." This is written in the Quran. May Allah have mercy on the soul of the beloved sheik. My goal was to live and die in the UAE but Allah had something bigger planned. Makkah is the hub of the Muslim world and just visiting is one the greatest of blessings, so how about living there for nine years?

We spent almost a decade in Makkah, living a peaceful family life, visiting the 'Haram" (the sacred sanctuary), and meeting Muslims from every place imaginable. My children attended public schools and eventually became fully bilingual (Arabic/English) with the help of daily tutoring and Quran classes offered at the neighborhood mosque.

The benefits of having raised my family in Makkah were invaluable. We drank the "Zamzam" water every day, performed Umrah in our free time, and visited Madina frequently. Two of my boys attended middle school at the Haram Institute (Mahad) learned from the likes of famous scholars, and observed the "hujjaj" often. (Hujjaj are the pilgrims who go to Makkah to perform traditional Islamic rituals)

Sadly, my mother passed away very unexpectedly in 2016 but I was even grateful to make "tawaf" on the night of her death. Although in a state of shock and completely grief-stricken, I had the care of friends and neighbors in addition to the support of the entire Muslim

"Ummah" or community, right in front of me. Every time I stood in front of the Kabbah (the black House inside the Haram), tears would flow reminding me of the many blessings we enjoyed. My colleagues, friends, and neighbors rallied around me at my lowest point and despite my sadness, I still felt overwhelmingly grateful for my life. That's when I learned the secret to happiness: never dwell on the past and don't allow yourself to be consumed with sadness. It's ok to have your feelings but important to keep them in check. From that terrible sad event of losing my mom, I decided to continue my own Quran lessons which helped strengthen my faith and stay focused on my hardest job: raising these children.

Eventually, in 2018, women were allowed to drive. I was one of the first to obtain an official Saudi driver's license in the city of Makkah. We had lived through a historical event, once again! This time it was a positive one and worked in my family's favor!

With that unprecedented change in Saudi law, my husband returned to North Carolina with our eldest child so that he could complete his senior year of high school and start college in the USA. Eventually, all 3 of the kids stayed with my husband in America, for their education, whereas I remained in Makkah with the younger 3. It was a challenge, but calling Makkah "home" made the split worth every sacrifice. We visited America every summer and they would also fly to Saudi for vacation throughout the year. I thought that I would live and die in Makkah and I was grateful for that. But once again we were about to live through an unprecedented historical event! My days in Makkah were numbered, so I had to once again re-evaluate my intentions, my goals, and my true aspirations.

8

COVID-19

March 9th, 2020 was the first day that the Saudi Ministry of Education declared that all education would be online, k-12, and university too. That is when I desperately started missing my children. They could not enter the Kingdom of Saudi Arabia and sadly, we could not leave. Youcef had purchased a ticket to come during his spring break. I thought he was en route until Turkish Airlines pulled him off the aircraft minutes before take off. Visas to Saudi Arabia were no longer honored as nobody would be allowed to enter. We were stuck and they were stuck, but this time I had enough faith to realize we were exactly where Allah wanted us to be, stuck separately in two different worlds with two very different time zones. Life would go on as many families had to make adjustments and once again, we hated something wherein there was much good that came from it.

My son, Yaqoob, graduated from his online high school and the best I could do was to have a cake delivered. My daughter, Fatima, graduated from high school, and family friends were kind enough to celebrate with her. Meanwhile, Youcef had been running my small business while I was in Saudi; an assortment of abayas and hijabs, "bakhoor" (incense), and carpets. Nobody was shopping in person anymore. Everything seemed to change in the blink of an eye. Thankfully we had the internet along with lots of applications to use for daily communication.

The only way out of this predicament was for me to quit my job and leave Saudi on a final exit visa. I held on tightly and stayed the course, resignation was not an option and all of us had hope that we would be united again either in Makkah or the USA. It was a test of patience. It was January 2021 when I received the call, my contract was not renewed and my job was ending. My director had done everything she could do but to no avail. I would not be teaching that spring semester but we stayed anyway for my children to finish their schooling and we fasted one last time in the month of "Ramadan" in Makkah. Every day was a gift, every prayer, every sip of Zamzam water. Finally, a solution had come but I was mourning the loss of the Holy City with each new day.

As my days were now free, I took advantage of this time. Now I had become a single married mom but my kids were a little more independent than ever before. Sometimes I would go shopping and ship more merchandise back home so that eventually my business would be fully stocked, ready for the post-Covid era and in-person shopping. I also joined a ladies' club and swam daily. These were some of the best days of my life, enjoying Makkah as any Muslim would. In fairness, I looked for jobs around Saudi but the opportunities were very limited due to Covid-19. So we made the best of our Ramadan and slowly emptied our beautiful villa. Once again we packed our entire lives into 8 suitcases and 4 backpacks knowing that was all we could take. A kind neighbor drove us to the airport and we processed our final exit visas, one by one. It was the second of "Shawwal" a day after Eid. I was ready once again to go back home.

9

A NEW CHAPTER BEGINS, ON MAY 13, 2021

It had been exactly five years to the day since my mother had passed away. The flight was bittersweet and finally, we arrived at Washington DC Dulles airport with 8 suitcases, 4 laptop bags, 4 backpacks, and 4 bottles of "Zamzam" water in tow. Just as he had done on my first return trip from Dubai, my husband was waiting, with flowers in hand, for the other half of his family. We stuffed the car to capacity and packed ourselves inside, making our way back home to North Carolina, once again. This time it was not the annual summer vacation, but rather a grand homecoming. The 5-hour drive felt like 5 minutes as we all took a deep sigh of relief. We had loved Saudi and always will, but Allah had taught me another valuable lesson: home is where the heart is. At that point in my life, home was where all my children could be together.

The tears were falling non-stop as we pulled up to a strange house; one that my younger 3 kids and I had never lived in before but had only seen videos of. We also met Fatima's two cats, the neighbors, and our dear friends. Over 18 months I had not hugged my children nor had my little ones hugged their older siblings. It was like a scene out of a movie, only we were not actors but rather, just ordinary human beings. My heart ached for the many people who had lost loved ones during COVID-19, who had lost their jobs, who had been separated from loved ones, and who had become depressed. I was grateful to be home again. I was eager to settle in. I was missing my life of 12 years in Saudi but I realized in that moment that everything happens for a reason, and Makkah had only been for a season.

At this point in May of 2021, Covid was under control and life was returning to normal again, especially here in the United States of America. Masks were a must and social distancing was still practiced, but people could now attend gatherings and school would be in-person that coming year. People were starting to feel more like themselves and not so afraid.

I decided to teach during the 2021-2022 academic year. It was not my plan to go back to teaching but to make private Islamic schooling affordable for my kids, this was my best chance. In August of 2021 we drove to school together each morning, the younger three kids and me. There were many changes to the red brick building and many more Muslims in the Triangle area. Shortly after my return to North Carolina in 1999, I noticed the magnificent newly-built white building, standing tall, directly facing the red brick building! It would eventually become the new mosque, housing their already established Islamic school, Al Iman while adding the Noor Quran Academy. Ironically the IAR complex had been thriving all those years despite 9/11, the economic crash, the wars the discrimination, and everything else. The Islamic Association of Raleigh, IAR, had become the hub for Muslims living in the Raleigh-Durham-Chapel Hill area. There is even a second campus now available in Durham. There are more than a dozen mosques in this part of North Carolina now, with several full-time Islamic schools. I had come full circle and was living out the next chapter of my travels, right at home in North Carolina.

10

EPILOGUE

It's now the summer of 2024 and life continues, with or without us. The lessons I have taken over the past twenty-six years are many, but here are a few of the important takeaways:

- Every action is by its intention, so make sure to keep your intentions good, always
- Actions are judged by their endings, so hold on tightly and finish up in a good way
- Patience is the key and the tool for success regarding most hardships in this life
- Keep your eyes on the prize and don't let people steal your dreams, you CAN do it!
- Invest in your children as you would invest in retirement, they'll pray for you after death
- Never underestimate any good deed for certainly what goes around, comes back around
- Be good to your parents, especially your mother, she is your paradise in this life
- Keep a list of goals, dreams, objectives, and bucket lists. You may never achieve them all but at least you'll stay busy trying!

As we move forward in life, tests and hardships will certainly come. The best gift we have ever been given is that of our faith. It will help you to overcome these tests, and it will keep you in check when life is good. Just as we travel through our mothers' bodies becoming "newborn babies", we are simply just travelers living our lives. Each day is a part of that journey. How blessed are we to have the Quran as our Guide? Prophet Muhammad (PBUH) as our model?

As we travel each day let's recognize that millions and billions of people have already gone ahead. How many millions or billions are coming after us? All we can take with us when we go are the good deeds we have done and eventually leave behind. We are all just traveling with a unique destiny, all of us have a final destination. Hopefully, our endings will be good ones. Amen.

Some Vocabulary (Arabic words put into English letters):
1. Shahada: the declaration of faith according to Muslims. When you take it, you're Muslim.
2. Tawheed: belief in the oneness of God
3. Takbeer: the saying "Allahu Akbar" meaning, "Allah is the greatest"
4. Allah: the Arabic word for God Almighty, who has no partners or any associates
5. Musafarah: the Arabic word for a female traveler
6. Ramadan - The 9th month of the Islamic calendar (lunar) wherein Muslims fast 29 or 30 days
7. Shawwal - the 10th month of the Islamic calendar (lunar) wherein Eid al Fitr is celebrated
8. Sheikh - Arabic word for a man who is knowledgeable in Islam or it could be an elderly man
9. Tawaf - Circumambulation around the Kabbah, a ritual done when entering the Holy Mosque

MUSAFIRAH: COMPREHENSION CHECK

- Why do you think she felt "like a newborn baby" after taking her "shahada?"
- Which continents has she lived on in her life?
- Where did she give birth?
- Who gave her the initial idea about Islam?
- What prompted her to leave the USA while living in Chicago?
- When did she say "...this is as good as it gets" in her life story?
- How many times does she move after taking her shahada?
- Why do you think she never talks about her family's reactions to converting?
- When did her mother pass away?
- Aside from Arabic, what language does she speak?

Bonus: What are the ages of her children after looking at the dates and time stamps?

Bonus: Where is she originally from? Why did she leave in the first place?

ANSWER KEY:
1. In Islam, it is said that once you become a Muslim, all your prior sins are forgiven. This means that you are starting your life over without any sins recorded. The common analogy of "feeling like a newborn baby" is often given by converts because they feel pure, fresh, clean, and innocent, like that of a baby, incapable of hurting anyone.
2. The continents are North America, Europe (France), and Asia (UAE and KSA) but she also vacationed in Africa! (Algeria)
3. She gave birth in North Carolina twice, and in the UAE twice, once in Chicago, and once in Saudi Arabia.
4. Her husband had first mentioned the idea of Islam to her, and he also helped her to understand some concepts by taking her to pick out books. It should be noted: that she researched the prohibitions first, and after she was convinced that Islam must be a divine religion based on scientific evidence, that's when she studied Islam.
5. Living in Chicago was freezing, lonely, and financially difficult. She also wanted her children to feel safe in a Muslim-majority land. Lastly, discrimination was still alive and well after the 9/11 events and she preferred her children avoid being treated suspiciously.
6. "As good as it gets" was her feeling in Chicago and she struggled emotionally for two and a half years. She wanted to stay where her husband could support them, but she longed for something better and took the chance by leaving for Saudi, with no regrets.
7. Moves: to Dubai, back to NC, to Sharjah, back to NC, to Emirates again (4 years), to NY state (briefly), and then to Chicago, to Taif, to Makkah, and back to NY. That's 10 times.
8. Her family has a right to their own personal and private feelings towards Aisha's conversion. It would not be fair or ethical to discuss that without their permission.

9. Sadly, her mom passed away very unexpectedly in May of 2016.
10. She speaks French. She started learning French in high school and then studied abroad in her junior year of college. Afterwards, she taught French for 2 years in NY.

Printed in Great Britain
by Amazon